Date: 6/29/18

J 947 BLA
Blake, Kevin,
Russia /

Russia

by Kevin Blake

Consultant: Karla Ruiz, MA
Teachers College, Columbia University
New York, New York

BEARPORT
PUBLISHING

New York, New York

Credits

Cover, © abadesign/Shutterstock and © VaLiza/Shutterstock; TOC, © Elena Blokhina/Shutterstock; 4, © Volodymyr Goinyk/Shutterstock; 5T, © Sergey Petrov/Shutterstock; 5B, © Lysogor Roman/Shutterstock; 7, © A_Vladimir/Shutterstock; 8, © kav38/iStock; 9T, © Gregory A. Pozhvanov/Shutterstock; 9B, © LeniKovaleva/Shutterstock; 10, © LuVo/iStock; 11, © Martynova Anna/Shutterstock; 12T, © Museum of History, Moscow, Russia/De Agostini Picture Library/A. Dagli Orti/Bridgeman Images; 12B, © Yaroslav Mishin/Shutterstock; 13, © Keith Levit/Shutterstock; 14, © Tass/UIG/Bridgeman Images; 15, © Sovfoto/UIG/AGE Fotostock; 16–17, © Vereshchagin Dmitry/Shutterstock; 17R, © Brian Kinney/Shutterstock; 18, © Aniriana/Shutterstock; 19, © Zeynep Ozyurek/iStock; 20L, © NASA/S.Dupuis/Alamy; 20R, Public Domain; 21T, Tallandier/Bridgeman; 21B, © NASA Archive/Alamy; 22, © Jackq/Dreamstime; 23T, © epa european pressphoto agency b.v./Alamy; 23B, © Alexander Podshivalov/Dreamstime; 24, © Idea Studio/Shutterstock; 25T, © mexrix/Shutterstock; 25B, © Chris Bull/Alamy; 26, © golubok/Shutterstock; 27TL, © Kletr/Shutterstock; 27TR, © AS Food studio/Shutterstock; 27B, © amberto4ka/Shutterstock; 28–29, © gans33/Shutterstock; 29R, © Andrey Arkusha/Shutterstock; 30T, © Asafta/Dreamstime and © schankz/Shutterstock; 30B, © Volodymyr Burdiak/Shutterstock; 31 (T to B), © liseykina/Shutterstock, © Steve Taylor/Alamy, © Africa Studio/Shutterstock, © VeronikaMaskova/Shutterstock, © Everett Historical/Shutterstock, and Public Domain; 32, © withGod/Shutterstock.

Publisher: Kenn Goin
Senior Editor: Joyce Tavolacci
Creative Director: Spencer Brinker
Design: Debrah Kaiser
Photo Researcher: Thomas Persano

Library of Congress Cataloging-in-Publication Data

Names: Blake, Kevin, 1978–author.
Title: Russia / by Kevin Blake.
Description: New York, New York : Bearport Publishing Company, Inc., [2017] | Series: Countries we come from | Includes bibliographical references and index. | Audience: Ages 5–8.
Identifiers: LCCN 2016038809 (print) | LCCN 2016039036 (ebook) | ISBN 9781684020560 (library) | ISBN 9781684021086 (ebook)
Subjects: LCSH: Russia (Federation)—Juvenile literature.
Classification: LCC DK510.23 .B53 2017 (print) | LCC DK510.23 (ebook) | DDC 947—dc23
LC record available at https://lccn.loc.gov/2016038809

For more information, write to Bearport Publishing Company, Inc., 45 West 21st Street, Suite 3B, New York, New York 10010. Printed in the United States of America.

10 9 8 7 6 5 4 3 2 1

Contents

This Is Russia

MAJESTIC

Full of Culture

HUGE

Russia is the largest country in the world.

It spans two **continents**—Europe and Asia!

Arctic Ocean

Russia

EUROPE

NORTH AMERICA

ASIA

Atlantic Ocean

Pacific Ocean

AFRICA

Pacific Ocean

SOUTH AMERICA

Indian Ocean

N

W   E

AUSTRALIA

S

Southern Ocean

ANTARCTICA

More than 143 million people live in Russia.

Huge mountains run through the country.

Russia's Mount Elbrus is the highest point in Europe!

Much of Russia is covered by flat grasslands called steppes.

steppe

There are huge areas of forests in Russia. In fact, the country has more forests than any other country in the world!

Russia has many different **climates**.

In some areas, such as Siberia, it's very cold.

The temperature can drop to an icy -89.8°F (-67.6°C)!

In other parts of the country, it's warm enough to swim.

Black Sea

Sochi is a Russian city on the coast of the Black Sea.

Russia has a long history.

For hundreds of years, mighty **tsars** ruled.

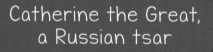

Catherine the Great, a Russian tsar

They helped make Russia very powerful.

Russian tsars lived in a huge building called the Winter Palace. It's now a museum.

In 1917, the Russian people got rid of the tsars.

Russia became the center of a new country called the Soviet Union.

The Soviet Union was also called the USSR. It was made up of 15 states, including Russia.

In 1991, the Soviet Union broke apart.
Russia became its own country again.

Moscow is the **capital** of Russia.
It's also Russia's largest city.

More than 12 million people live there.

Saint Petersburg is Russia's second-largest city.

Most people in Russia speak Russian.

Russian uses different letters than the English language.

This is how you write and say *hi* in Russian:

привет
(pree-VYEHT)

19

Did you know that the first person in space was Russian?

His name is Yuri Gargarin.

Yuri Gargarin went to space in 1961.

However, Laika, a Russian dog, got sent to space four years before Yuri!

Russia put the first **satellite** in space, too. It was called Sputnik 1.

Russians love music and dance!

Moscow's Bolshoi ballet is one of the most famous in the world.

Dancers leap to songs written by famous Russian **composers**.

Folk dancing is also popular in Russia.

Russians are also big fans of ice hockey.

Some children grow up playing on frozen ponds.

Whack! The puck flies through the air.

What other sports do Russians enjoy? Soccer, basketball, and chess!

There are many delicious Russian foods.

People enjoy different kinds of pancakes.

Russians also like salty fish eggs called caviar.

Soup made from beets and cabbage is eaten on cold nights.

What else is special about Russia?
The country is home to Lake Baikal.

It's the largest and deepest lake in the world!

More than 28 million people visit Russia each year.

Fast Facts

Capital city: Moscow

Population of Russia: More than 143 million

Main language: Russian

Money: Ruble

Major religion: Russian Orthodox

Neighboring countries include: Kazakhstan, China, Ukraine, Belarus, Finland, Latvia, Poland, and Mongolia

Cool Fact: Russia's most famous animal is the Siberian tiger. It's the largest cat in the world!

Glossary

capital (KAP-uh-tuhl) a city where a country's government is based

climates (KLYE-mits) typical weather patterns in an area

composers (kuhm-POH-zurz) people who write music

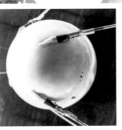

continents (KON-tuh-nuhnts) the world's seven large land masses

satellite (SAT-uh-*lite*) a spacecraft that circles Earth

tsars (ZARZ) kings or queens of Russia

Index

Read More

Bartell, Jim. *Russia (Blastoff! Readers: Exploring Countries).* Minnetonka, MN: Bellwether (2010).

Hunt, Jilly. *Russia (Countries Around the World).* Portsmouth, NH: Heinemann (2012).

Learn More Online

To learn more about Russia, visit
www.bearportpublishing.com/CountriesWeComeFrom

About the Author

Kevin Blake lives in Providence, Rhode Island, with his wife, Melissa, son, Sam, and daughter, Ilana. His great-grandmother, Sarah, came from Russia to the United States when she was a little girl.